TO THE LIMIT

Terrifying Storms

Jim Pipe

First published in 2014 by Franklin Watts

Copyright © Franklin Watts 2014

Franklin Watts
338 Euston Road
London NW1 3BH

Franklin Watts Australia
Level 17/207 Kent Street
Sydney, NSW 2000

Produced for Franklin Watt by White-Thomson Publishing Ltd

www.wtpub.co.uk
+44 (0) 843 208 7460

Edited and designed by Paul Manning

A CIP catalogue record for this book is available from the British Library.

Dewey no: 551.5'5
Hardback ISBN: 978 1 4451 3421 5
Library eBook ISBN: 978 1 4451 3601 1

Printed in China

Franklin Watts is a division of Hachette Children's Books,
an Hachette UK company.
www.hachette.co.uk

Picture credits:
Front cover: Photolibrary/Hank Delespinasse; 3, 5, Mike Hollingshead/Science Faction/
Corbis; 6a, Shutterstock/Jan Schuler; 6b, Hyperion Books.com; 7, Dorothy Pugh; 8, Rafiqur
Rahman/Reuters/Corbis; 8 (map), Stefan Chabluk; 9, Rafiqur Rahman/ Reuters/Corbis;
10 background, Shutterstock/Daniel Loretto; 11l, Expert Collision; 11r, National Oceanic
and Atmospheric Administration/Department of Commerce; 12a, Shutterstock/VR Photos;
12b, Wikimedia Commons/Historic NWS Collection; 14, Reuters/CORBIS; 14 inset,
Shutterstock/jam4travel; 15, Corbis/Mike Theiss; 16, Bisson Bernard/Corbis Sygma;
17r, NOAA/Satellite and Information Service; 18, Wikimedia Commons/USCG; 19,
Corbis/Smiley N. Pool; 20, Photolibrary/White Fox; 21, Cambridge Bay Weather; 22,
Mrcricket48; 23, AFP/Getty Images; 24, Corbis/Mick Tsikas; 25, Corbis/Morton Beebe; 26,
Shutterstock/Amy Johansson; 27l, Shutterstock/Neon Tl; 27r, Shutterstock/AlexKalashnikov.

Every attempt has been made to clear copyright. Should there be any inadvertent
omission please apply to the publisher for rectification.

Hey there! Before reading this book, it's really important for you to know
that the activities shown are meant for you to enjoy reading and for no other
purpose. The activities depicted are really dangerous; trying to do them could
hurt or even kill you. They should only be done by professionals who have had a
lot of training and, even then they are still really dangerous and can cause injury.
So we don't encourage you to try any of these activities. Just enjoy the read!

Contents

Into the Hurricane

Storms on land are scary enough, but full-blown hurricanes at sea are terrifying. Up to 960 kilometres across, these spiralling monsters bring winds faster than a speeding train and giant waves that can smash a ship to pieces in seconds.

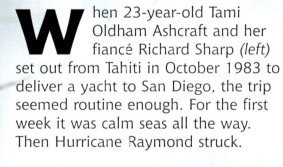

When 23-year-old Tami Oldham Ashcraft and her fiancé Richard Sharp *(left)* set out from Tahiti in October 1983 to deliver a yacht to San Diego, the trip seemed routine enough. For the first week it was calm seas all the way. Then Hurricane Raymond struck.

Soon the yacht was being pounded by 260-kph winds and waves the size of a five-storey building. Tami screamed to Richard, 'Is this as bad as it's going to get?' He replied, 'We'll tell our grandchildren about this. We're going to make it.' Clipping himself to a lifeline, Richard told Tami to go below. Moments later, the boat rolled over, then catapulted end-over-end through the air.

▲ *All sailors in the Tropics dread the huge storms known as hurricanes or cyclones that sweep across the Pacific during the summer months.*

Alone at sea

Tami woke up 27 hours later. Her head was covered in blood. The last thing she remembered was Richard's scream as the boat flipped over. Though the storm had passed, Richard had vanished into the dark ocean. His safety line had snapped and he had been swept overboard. Tami was alone.

Stunned

For two days Tami was too stunned to act. But the terrifying storm which had robbed her of her partner had not destroyed her will to survive.

▼ *In the USA, the storm surge from Hurricane Katrina in August 2005 was one of the most powerful ever recorded. An estimated 1,863 people lost their lives in the hurricane and resulting floods in New Orleans.*

Tami built a makeshift sail and mast and figured out a course to Hawaii. After 42 days, she sailed into the Big Island's Hilo Harbor. Today Tami lives in the San Juan Islands in Washington State. She continues to sail.

STORM SURGE

One of the most destructive effects of a hurricane is the storm surge that devastates coastal areas when it reaches land. As the winds circle around the storm, a huge mound of water piles up at its centre, gaining strength as the hurricane hurtles towards the coast.

A Drowned World

If you think it's wet where you live, try Bangladesh. The heavy rains that fall here each year cause far more damage than any wind. In 2007, the country was devastated by floods. Without proper defences or rescue services, 4,000 people died, and 5 million others were forced to flee their homes.

A Bangladeshi man fetches drinking water for his family on an air-filled rubber float during the 2007 floods.

Many people in Bangladesh have never heard of global warming. Yet they have to live with the effects of it every day of their lives. In the dry season, farmers like Shahidul Mullah hurry to prepare for the rains. But things are getting harder: 'Every year it gets warmer and there are more storms. The monsoon doesn't come on time.'

In the summer of 2007, the rains poured down. At first, most people weren't too worried – heavy rains are normal in the monsoon season. But as rivers burst their banks, large areas of the country were covered in a giant sheet of water. The rains also caused landslides: dozens of homes were buried under mud and hundreds lost their lives.

The cyclone strikes

To make matters worse, coastal areas were hit by Cyclone Sidr. Its 260-kph winds whipped up a six-metre surge that swept across the tiny island of Ashar Char. Local fisherman Khaleque Howlander desperately tried to get his family and friends to high ground. But the huge tide caught up with them. Khaleque only saved his family by using empty water jugs as floats and tying his children to a tree branch with a sari.

The next morning, Khaleque found the bodies of many of his neighbours. He was devastated: 'Here, there are always cyclones, but I have never seen anything like that before. We have lost everything.'

▼ *Straddling the fertile delta of the Ganges and Brahmaputra Rivers, Bangladesh is regularly devastated by floods and cyclones.*

RISING SEA LEVELS

As polar ice caps melt due to global warming, sea levels rise, making life tougher then ever for people living in low-lying coastal regions. 'The water has always been our enemy but also a source of life,' says one Bangladeshi man. 'Now, the water just takes land away from me; it hardly gives me anything in exchange.'

Gliding to Disaster

On the ground, violent hailstorms can leave roofs and car windscreens shattered, crops flattened and livestock lying dead in the fields. But high up in the clouds, the swirling updrafts of icy air can sometimes pose an even more deadly danger…

In the 1920s, the peak of Wasserkuppe in Germany's Rhön Mountains was a popular place to fly gliders. Pilots from all over the world were drawn by the air currents there that lifted their planes high into the sky. Nothing seemed out of the ordinary when five German glider pilots set out for a day's flying.

⚠ Hailstorms are a potentially lethal danger to aircraft. A big hailstone can reach a speed of more than 200 kph – easily enough to punch a hole right through a glider's fragile wings.

Hailstorm warning

Not long after take-off, the pilots saw the first warning signs of a hailstorm on the horizon. At first, they thought they could ride it out – but they were mistaken.

As the winds grew stronger and stronger, the pilots had no choice but to bale out and let the gliders go. But instead of falling to earth, they found themselves sucked upwards into the storm by the powerful air currents. Each time they dropped, the winds swept them up again. Soon all five men were wrapped in heavy layers of ice.

Human hailstones

Finally, the storm let go of its victims – and the five human hailstones plummeted 2 kilometres to the ground. Four died, either frozen to death or killed by the impact. Incredibly, one pilot survived after the cocoon of ice wrapped around his body broke his fall.

WHAT IS HAIL?

Hail is made up of tiny clumps of ice which are swept into freezing thunderclouds by strong upward-moving air currents. The pellets of ice continue to be tossed around until eventually they become too heavy to be supported by the cloud's updraft and fall to earth.

◄ Hailstorms are especialy common in the USA and cause widespread damage to property.

◄ Hailstones can be anything up to 15 centimetres in diameter.

Bolt from Above

Lightning is one of the most spectacular sights in nature. A flash of lightning streaks across the sky at speeds up to 150,000 kph, heating up the air around it to a sizzling 27,000°C – three times the temperature on the Sun's surface. No wonder a lightning strike can be deadly… but not always!

► Tall buildings are especially vulnerable to lightning strikes. This photograph taken in 1902 shows lightning striking the Eiffel Tower in Paris, France.

◄ Lightning is produced when tiny particles of ice collide in the sky, generating an electrical charge. The energy builds up until the positive charge in the air connects with the negative charge of an object on the ground – typically a church spire, a tree or a metal object. Zap! Lightning strikes!

They say lightning never strikes the same place twice. Tell that to Roy Sullivan (right). During his 36-year career as a park ranger in Virginia, USA, Roy was struck by lightning seven times!

- **Strike 1** In 1942, Roy was inside a lookout tower, sheltering from a thunderstorm. After it was struck by lightning seven or eight times, Roy decided to run for it. Bad mistake. A bolt shot through Roy's leg, blasting his toenail off and burning a hole in his shoe.

- **Strike 2** Twenty-seven years later, a lightning strike burned off Ray's eyebrows and knocked him unconscious. He was driving a truck at the time, which should have protected him.

- **Strike 3** In 1970, another strike burned Roy's shoulder while he walked across his yard to collect his post. 'It was like being cooked inside your skin,' he said later.

- **Strike 4** In 1972, a lightning bolt set Roy's hair on fire. By now he was getting paranoid. Was someone – or something – out to get him?

- **Strike 5** A year later, Roy was out on patrol when another lightning bolt set light to his hair and knocked his left shoe off.

- **Strike 6** A lightning bolt in 1976 injured his ankle. Roy said he saw the cloud trying to follow him. He tried to run away, but there was no escape!

- **Strike 7** Roy was zapped again as he went fishing. Shortly after, a bear tried to steal his fish, but Roy beat him off with a branch.

LIGHTNING SAFETY

- Avoid angling and golf – both hobbies use metal objects that can attract lightning.
- Water attracts lightning, so outdoor swimming is a bad idea if there's a storm nearby.
- If your hair stands up in a storm, lightning may be heading your way. Get inside quickly!
- Once you're indoors, stay away from windows and doors, and avoid anything electrical, especially telephones.

Chasing Tornadoes

A tornado, or 'twister', is a vicious funnel-shaped storm that hops across the ground, flinging cars about and smashing houses to pieces. Most people run for cover when they hear the jet-engine roar of a tornado approaching, but stormchasers do the opposite: they risk life and limb to get as close as they can!

▼ *A tornado is a terrifying force of nature, generating winds of up to 480 kph. Each year, some 1,200 tornadoes occur in the US, killing around 70 people and injuring another 1,500.*

According to stormchaser Matt Biddle, 'Some people follow football teams, others follow tornadoes'. But storm-chasing is for serious fans only. There's real danger from hailstones, gale-force winds, lightning, flooding and flying debris.

Often there are disappointments – it's not unusual to drive hundreds of kilometres in a weekend without ever catching sight of a 'twister'. But for dedicated stormchasers, the thrill of experiencing nature's fury at first hand makes it all worthwhile!

Waterspout

One storm researcher, Joe Golden, persuaded a friend to fly a plane through a waterspout, a type of tornado that occurs over water, near Key West, Florida, USA. He remembers gripping his seat, 'with white knuckles,' while the pilot struggled to keep the plane from spinning out of control.

As they flew into the waterspout, Golden was tossed around the tiny plane like a rag doll. He recalls how the vibrations 'rattled my teeth.' But in less than a second they passed right through the waterspout and out the other side, collecting important data on the way. And you thought scientists pottered about in the lab all day!

DID YOU KNOW?

• In 1880, a tornado in Missouri picked up a house and carried it 19 kilometres.
• Most tornadoes only last a few minutes, so they're very hard to track.
• The tail end of a tornado (known as the 'bear's cage') does most of the damage.
• Some tornadoes are invisible! That's partly why tornadoes are measured by the amount of damage they do, rather than by size or wind speed.

▶ These houses were flattened by a 'twister' in 'Tornado Alley' in the central USA.

◀ A stormchaser films an approaching thunderstorm in the central USA. A tornado struck moments after this photo was taken.

Eye of the Storm

The Caribbean Sea has had more than its fair share of stormy weather. But no one was prepared for the savage force of Hurricane Mitch when it struck in 1998. One survivor said it sounded like 'a thousand express trains roaring through a tunnel'. Mitch was one of the deadliest storms in recent history, leaving 18,000 people dead or missing.

▶ *Poor people like these Honduran villagers are the worst affected by any natural disaster. Hurricane Mitch left villages flattened, roads and bridges destroyed and whole areas without electricity. Later, many houses were rebuilt but the economy was shattered and crops took years to recover.*

From the air a hurricane can be an impressive, even a beautiful sight. On the ground the impact is terrible. Laura Isabel Arriola was living with her family in Honduras when Hurricane Mitch hit the coastline, creating a huge wall of water that flattened her house and many others.

Rising waters

Laura and her family took refuge in a neighbour's house, but the rising waters ripped through the house. Soon Laura found herself cut off from her family. She never saw them alive again. 'I swam and swam' she said later, 'trying to get somewhere dry, but then I realised I was already in the sea.'

▶ *In a hurricane, the spin of the Earth causes the storm to swirl around a centre known as the 'eye', creating 285-kph winds.*

MITCH THE MONSTER

Hurricane Mitch started life as a tropical storm, but warm air rising from the sea turned it into a monster. After hurtling across the ocean, Mitch headed inland, dropping record rainfall and causing flooding throughout Central America.

Scared and alone

Swept far from land, Laura clung for four hours to some floating palm branches. Then, using debris in the water, she made a raft for herself. For six days, she lived on coconuts and pineapples that floated by. Rough seas constantly battered her raft. Twice she was plunged into the water. She felt scared and alone.

On the sixth day, she saw a duck swimming past. In her desperation, Laura cried out, 'Little duck, send a message I'm alive.' Her prayers were answered. A few hours later she was spotted by a plane flying overhead and picked up by a helicopter.

Atlantic Rescue

A helicopter search-and-rescue team consists of four persons, including the pilot and co-pilot. Once the helicopter arrives at the scene, a rescue swimmer is winched down to pick up survivors. The winch operator also takes care of survivors needing first aid.

When a storm warning goes out, helicopter crews need to be prepared for all weathers. But even the most experienced rescue crews can be shocked at the rough conditions they encounter during an Atlantic storm.

> 'We were stunned by the size of the waves. They just got bigger and bigger.'

In May 2007, a US coastguard helicopter was called into action after a sailing vessel, the *Sean Seymour 2*, capsized in the North Atlantic. Forced to abandon ship in atrocious weather, the crew had managed to haul themselves onto a tiny life raft, but were being battered by huge waves. Time was short.

Rescue swimmer

By the time the helicopter arrived, the raft was hard to spot in the deep canyons of water. The plan was to lower crew member Drew Dazzo into the raging sea to pick up the survivors. But it was tough going: 'We were stunned by the size of the waves,' Drew said later. 'They just got bigger and bigger.'

Frayed cable

Eventually Drew had to be lowered three times to pick up the survivors. What the crew didn't realise was that the hoist cable was starting to fray. If it had snapped, the chopper would have been forced to head for home, leaving Drew and any remaining survivors still in the water.

◀ *Following Hurricane Katrina in 2005, a woman is hoisted from the flood waters by a military helicopter in New Orleans, USA. Nearly a week after the storm struck, residents were still being rescued from rooftops across the city.*

Blizzard Survival

In the frozen polar regions, snowstorms called blizzards can appear from nowhere, hurling snow and ice at you and sucking the heat right out of your body. Drop a glove and your hand freezes solid in minutes. Yet peoples such as the Inuit of Greenland have been surviving Arctic blizzards for 15,000 years.

▼ *Inuit hunters build a dome-shaped shelter called an igloo using specially shaped blocks of snow.*

Over the centuries the Inuit have learned to adapt to some of the most hostile weather conditions on Earth. In the daily battle to survive, nothing is wasted. Reindeer skins make warm clothes. Seal-skin jackets protect against the icy Arctic winds. Fur boots are lined with moss and dry grass for extra insulation.

Surviving a blizzard

But even the Inuit hunters can be caught out by a sudden blizzard. The driving snow causes 'whiteouts', when the air is so thick with snow you can't tell the ground from the sky. The best way to survive is to build a shelter – fast. An igloo *(facing page)* is surprisingly warm inside. With temperatures as low as −30°C even in summer, it needs to be!

Frostbite

The Inuit have also learned how to cope with other problems such as frostbite. A common trick among Arctic peoples is to wrinkle up their faces now and then to see if there are any stiff patches. These are a warning sign of mild frostbite, called 'frost-nip'.

Goggles

Snowblindness, caused by looking at bright white snow for too long, can seriously damage your eyes. While modern explorers wear dark goggles or sunglasses, Inuit peoples carve snow goggles out of caribou antlers. These have a narrow slit that protects their eyes from the glare of the snow.

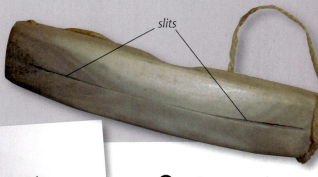

slits

BUILT FOR THE COLD

The Inuit have a key advantage to survive in the Arctic – they're built for the cold. Their naturally short bodies conserve heat. Thick pads on their cheeks protect them against cold, while their heavy eyelids protect against the glare of the sun.

◣ Inuit snow goggles made from caribou antler, with caribou sinew for a strap.

Cauldron of Dust

In September 2009, a giant orange dust cloud 500 kilometres wide and more than 1,000 kilometres long settled over Australia, 'blacking out' dozens of towns and cities. Swirling 100 kph winds had carried more than 16 million tonnes of dust from the deserts of Central Australia.

⬤ *The Sydney Harbour Bridge during the 2009 Australian dust storm. Many smoke alarms were set off by the dust, and flights were cancelled across the city. Not surprisingly, sales of face masks soared.*

Shortly before the dust storm hit Sydney, John White was driving along a remote road in the Simpson Desert when a sand dune collapsed under his car. The car rolled over, trapping him inside.

Squeezing out through the passenger window, John set off an emergency signal to alert the rescue services. But the sand kept on blowing. The track he had been driving on was no longer visible. 'There could have been people driving either side of me and they would never have seen me,' John said later.

Lucky escape

The nearest town was Birdsville, some 200 kilometres away. Though the emergency services had picked up his distress signal, the dust storm blocked attempts to reach John by plane and helicopter. Meanwhile, little by little, his car was being buried. John said, 'I spent most of the day pushing dirt out so I didn't get buried myself'.

Determined Birdsville policeman Neale McShane drove for hours through the horror storm, and 10 hours after the accident, John was rescued. He knew he was lucky to be alive. 'A couple of times I really thought that all they might find was some bleached bones out there with the dingoes.'

DESERT STORM

In parts of the Gobi Desert, the constant strong winds shift even the biggest sand dunes by about 50 metres a year. In 2006, fierce winds in the Gobi Desert whipped up an incredible 300,000 tonnes of sand, then dumped it on the city of Beijing 1,600 kilometres away, covering the city in clouds of choking dust.

▼ Chinese cyclists wear face masks during a dust storm in the northeastern city of Shenyang in March 2004.

The Diablo Effect

After months of dry weather, the impact of a wildfire can be devastating. Fanned, by a scorching wind such as California's notorious 'Diablo', a small blaze can soon turn into a raging firestorm that devours everything in its path.

The day a firestorm swept through the Oakland hills near San Francisco in the USA in 1991, Karen McClung was outside playing soccer. By the evening, everything she owned had been destroyed, apart from her soccer kit and some photo albums which her daughter had grabbed before fleeing the house. When Karen saw the smoking remains of her home two days later, 'it looked like the moon – it was all black and grey and burned.'

▼ In February 2009 firefighters In Australia faced raging wildfires all over the country. Some had been started deliberately by arsonists, but they were quickly spread by the hot, dry winds that swept across the continent.

'Diablo' wind

Temperatures were already in the 40s when the hot, dry Diablo winds raced in at speeds over 100 kph, swirling through bone-dry brush and pines. A single hot ember from a smouldering fire blew into a tree, which burst into flames.

Cars exploded as the firestorm swept through the hills. One resident described the chaos: 'As things burn up, you lose track of where you are. A lot of landmarks were destroyed.'

Out of control

Before long the inferno was out of control and firefighters were fighting for their lives. At its peak, the blaze destroyed 1 home every 11 seconds. Some 3,500 homes were burned down and 25 people were killed. Diablo winds had caused the most destructive wildfire in US history.

▶ *Charred remains of a car destroyed in the Oaklands firestorm of 1991.*

WINDS OF DEATH

The freak windstorms that blow onto California's coastline have long been a threat to the region. In 1850, the blast of hot air that swept over the town of Santa Barbara killed calves, rabbits and birds where they stood and baked the fruit on the trees. No one knows when or where these deadly winds will strike next.

Raining Animals!

Heard the expression 'raining cats and dogs'? Well, no one has yet seen cats and dogs falling from the sky – but strong winds have been known to sweep frogs, spiders, fish and even turtles and snakes into the air!

The most common animals to drop out of the sky are fish and frogs. Amazingly, some animals even survive the fall, but most are found frozen to death or wrapped in a layer of ice. Some scientists believe the freaky rainfalls could be caused by mini-waterspouts or tornadoes, which can be strong enough to suck up anything in their path.

'BIZARRE FALLING OBJECTS'

If you think frog or fish showers are strange, how about these 'BFOs'?

- On 1 August 1869 an unidentified animal (thought to be a cow) fell in California. It appeared to have been ripped into tiny pieces.
- In 1894, jellyfish fell from the sky in Bath, England.
- On 11 July 2007, worms dropped from the sky in Jennings, Louisiana, USA.

⏶ Showers of frogs and fish have been reported in countries all over the world. Most animal showers seem to occur during storms, but occasionally creatures have been known to drop out of a clear blue sky.

Wriggling worms

In 2007, Eleanor Beal was crossing the street in Jennings, Louisiana, USA, when something dropped out of the sky with a thud – a clump of wriggling worms! Around the same time, a waterspout was spotted over a river less than 8 kilometres away. Could the worms have been sucked up by the spout, carried through the air and dumped on land?

Silver shower

Following a thunderstorm in August 2000, a silver shower of baby fish rained down on a street in Great Yarmouth in the UK. Several gardens were strewn with the 5 centimetre-long sprats. 'I knew nobody would believe me, so I got my neighbours to have a look' said an amazed witness. 'One of them had their garden shed covered in fish. It was quite extraordinary.'

With global warming likely to bring more stormy and unpredictable weather, should we expect more reports of 'Bizarre Falling Objects'?

▼ *Danger – falling tadpoles! In June 2009 a 55-year-old man in Nanao, Japan, found himself caught in a slimy shower. Looking closer, he found that nearby cars were covered in more than a hundred squished tadpoles. After his story was reported in the news, many other people all over Japan reported similar findings.*

▲ *Freak showers of fish are not as unusual as you might think.*

Would You Survive?

Could you cope with a cyclone or keep calm during a tornado?
Check how storm-proof you are with this easy-to-answer quiz.

1 The car you're in is swamped by a flash flood. Do you:

   a Shut all doors and windows and hope that a team of rescue divers is on the way.

   b Get out as quickly as possible. Use the window if the door won't open. Then head for high ground.

   c Wait until the car sinks, then take a deep breath and swim to the surface.

2 An avalanche is hurtling down the mountain towards you. Do you:

   a Try to outrun it, screaming 'Catch me if you can!'

   b Struggle to stay on top of the snow using a freestyle swimming motion.

   c Start digging a hole to hide in.

3 What's the best way to avoid being struck by lightning?

   a Find a high place and wave something metallic in the air.

   b Get inside as quickly as possible and avoid touching anything electrical.

   c Hide under a tree and wait for the storm to pass.

4 A hurricane is on its way. Do you:

   a Wait until it arrives, then run outside to experience the awesome power of nature.

   b Evacuate as soon as possible. Head for high ground away from the coast or rivers.

   c Stay inside and take the occasional peek through the window to see what is happening outside.

5 You're walking out in the open when you're caught by a sudden blizzard. What's your best chance of survival?

   a Struggle on through the storm and hope it'll blow over in a few minutes.

   b Find shelter as soon as possible out of the wind or failing that, dig a snow cave.

   c Stay put and call for help on your mobile phone.

CHECK YOUR SCORE

Mostly a's You won't last long with these crazy tactics!

Mostly b's Good choices – you're a born survivor.

Mostly c's A brave attempt, but you've chosen some risky options.

Glossary

algae simple types of non-flowering plant

antler large horn on the head of a reindeer

arsonist person who deliberately damages property

blizzard a severe snowstorm

calf a baby cow

canyon a deep valley

cauldron large bowl in which things are heated

chopper slang name for a helicopter

cocoon a protective outer case

cyclone a type of violent tropical storm in which wind rotates around a central 'eye'

delta the mouth of a river

dingo a wild dog found in Australia

ember a small piece of burning or glowing material

firestorm a raging fire which is fanned by the air around it

frostbite a skin condition caused by extreme cold

global warming rise in temperature caused by levels of greenhouse gases in the atmosphere

hurricane a type of violent tropical storm

igloo an Inuit shelter made from blocks of ice

insulation padding designed to keep out the cold

livestock farm animals such as cattle or pigs

monsoon type of wind that brings rain when blowing from the south-west

pellet a small hard lump of something

polar relating to the area around the North or South Poles

reindeer a deer with large **antlers**

sari garment worn by Indian women

sprat a small sea fish

storm surge a 'wall of water' created by a hurricane

stormchaser person who travels from place to place in search of storms

tadpole a baby frog

tornado a violent wind that forms a funnel shape

twister see **tornado**

updraft an upward-moving air current

waterspout type of **tornado** that occurs over water

wildfire a rapidly spreading fire

winch a lifting device, usually operated by turning a handle

windstorm a storm with strong winds but little or no rain

Websites

http://dsc.discovery.com/convergence/tornado/tornado.html
Create your own virtual tornado and see what happens!

www.extremescience.com/weatherport.htm
Facts and figures, pictures and useful links to online resources.

www.nasa.gov/mission_pages/hurricanes/main/index.html
Watch hurricanes from space at this NASA site.

Note to parents and teachers

Every effort has been made by the Publishers to ensure that the web sites in this book are suitable for children, that they are of the highest educational value, and that they contain no inappropriate or offensive material. However, because of the nature of the Internet, it is impossible to guarantee that the contents of these sites will not be altered. We strongly advise that Internet access is supervised by a responsible adult.

Index